LUCIANA FISHER

beneath the surface

Luciana Fisher's
Beneath the Surface Fund
for Survivorship & Neurodivergence

CONTENTS

. . . .

1. The Silent Storms We Sail *(Resilience and Growth)* 13
   The Big Sea That I Sail
   Makeup
   Ignliv with YdsLexya
   Urgency
   Memories of an Inner Child
   The Power of Gratitude

. . . .

2. Mirrors and Shadows *(Identity and Self-Discovery)* 44
   Identity: Under You
   Note to Self
   The Paradox of Time
   Who Are We?
   Languages

. . . .

3. The Threads That Bind Us *(Relationships and Connection)* 74
   Mission
   Tend to What Matters
   What Was Left Unsaid
   What Love Is
   Connection
   Stitch
   Spidey

. . . .

ACKNOWLEDGEMENTS

To those who have shaped my journey, your presence—whether fleeting or constant—has left an indelible mark. To my family, friends, and readers: thank you for your love, encouragement, and belief in the power of words.

To my editor, collaborators, and fellow creatives who have guided me with wisdom and kindness, you've helped me find clarity in vulnerability.

To those who shared their stories with me or inspired these pages, I am eternally grateful.

Finally, the ones who gave me the courage to write again this collection carries pieces of your encouragement in every line. Thank you for believing in me.

LUCIANA FISHER

To My Inner Child,
Who always wanted to write—
Here we are.
Thank you for never letting go of the dream,
for the hints, whispers, nudges, and screams through the years, and for
believing that words could heal and connect.
This is for you.

PREFACE

Beneath the Surface began as fragments of thoughts scribbled in journals, moments captured in the margins of everyday life. These poems emerged from my deepest joys, quiet fears, and the lessons life whispered— sometimes more like shouted—in my direction.

This collection is an exploration, a reckoning, and an embrace. It's about navigating life's complexities, celebrating its fleeting beauty, and finding strength in vulnerability.

I am reflecting on my story, but I also invite you to reflect on your own. May these words meet you where you are, offering solace, courage, or even just a moment to pause. Thank you for letting me share this journey with you.

ABOUT THE AUTHOR

Luciana Fisher is a poet, writer, and storyteller whose work explores love, loss, identity, and transformation themes. Born in Brazil and living in the United States, Luciana draws from personal experience, keen observation, and deep reflection, blending her multicultural background with an intimate exploration of human emotions.

Currently pursuing a degree in Social Sciences with a concentration in Economics from New York University, Luciana rekindled her passion for poetry after finding solace and purpose in writing after being diagnosed with cancer. Her work has been featured in symposiums and publications, and Beneath the Surface marks her debut poetry collection.

When she's not writing, Luciana enjoys reading and performing her pieces around New York, immersing herself in nature, and spending time with her beloved dogs, Stitch and Spidey. A lifelong explorer of storytelling in all its forms, she believes in the transformative power of vulnerability to heal, connect, and inspire. Through her words, Luciana invites readers to embrace their own truths and discover the beauty of authenticity.

Each poem tells a story, yet each holds a story within its lines. Thank you for taking the time to look behind the lines with me. I hope you enjoy the journey.
— **Luciana Fisher.**

WHY GO BEHIND THE LINES?

The Behind the Lines pages is my way of inviting you into the conversation and my creative process. Poetry is deeply personal, but it also thrives on connection. By sharing the inspiration, craft, and themes behind each poem, I hope to create a space where you can explore not just my journey, but your own. Writing, to me, is a dialogue—a way to leave a mark and to connect with others through the timeless power of storytelling. Let these lyrical prose and poetry reflections be an open door to engage with the words, the emotions, and the truths that resonate with you.

Should you feel compelled to write to me, please do. I would love to hear from you. You can email me at: *hello@lucianafisher.com* or find me on IG: *@lbfisher*

In vulnerability lies unimaginable power,
To heal, to connect, to break through the mould.

THE SILENT STORMS WE SAIL
Resilience and Growth

The Big Sea That I Sail

The sea
I sail
Is silent.
So silent—it almost fooled me.
It required no license or permit.
You see,
The. C. that. I. sail.
Is. silent.

It cares not —
If I sail or sink,
Seizing,
At high speed,
Every cell inside of me.

You see,
More women

Will rise to C —
But our routes will resemble none.
For the big sea
We sail
Is silent,
And the crew,
A brave army —
Of one.

THE BIG SEA THAT I SAIL
BEHIND THE LINES:

In The Big Sea That I Sail, I aim to capture the isolation and resilience required to navigate life's silent battles. The nautical imagery reflects the ebb and flow of waves, symbolizing the shifting tides of fear and strength. The poem's structure mimics this rhythm, with deliberate pauses and pacing to pull readers into the uncertainty of uncharted waters. Repetition emphasizes the cyclical nature of these struggles, while the metaphor of "the crew of one" highlights the solitude of personal battles.

The sea is silent because, for many, these battles—like cancer—sneak in quietly, unnoticed, yet they can upend life completely. The line "It required no license or permit" reflects how uninvited and uncontrollable this journey feels—no one chooses it, and no one can truly prepare for it.

"It cares not—if I sail or sink" conveys the cruel indifference of the challenge. I personified the sea here to make it feel like an adversary, a force that seizes control. The phrase "Seizing, at high speed, every cell inside of me" mirrors the invasive, rapid nature of cancer and how it takes over the body without pause.

The poem also explores the dual nature of water: as a challenge when facing the vast, unpredictable sea, but also as a source of healing and comfort. During chemotherapy, sleepless nights often found me in the bathtub, using water to regulate my body temperature. It was there in solitude and darkness that this piece came to me.

When I wrote "More women will rise to C—but our routes will resemble none," I was thinking of the shared, yet deeply unique journeys women take through cancer or other hardships. No two paths are the same, even when we face similar storms.

The title itself plays on the homophony between C and Sea, adding an open-ended symbolism. For me, C reflects my battle with cancer, but its meaning is now yours to define. It might represent cancer, change, challenges, or something else entirely.

This poem invites readers to reflect on their own storms and how they navigate them. It's not just about isolation—it's also about the resilience we carry within, often without realizing it. The Big Sea That I Sail is my personal reflection, but I hope it resonates with anyone who has faced a challenge they never chose.

To my fellow warriors,
Who sail through storms they never chose —
May you find strength in every wave,
Hope in the darkest skies,
And the courage to keep rewriting your story.
This journey does not define us,
But it reveals the resilience within us.
You are not alone.
— **L.F**

Reader Reflection:

What storms in your life have tested your resilience, and how did you find the strength to sail through them?

Makeup

I no longer wear make-up.
Nor on my skin,
Cheeks, nose, or chin,
    But on my lips.
No, I do not use make up.
—*You can touch.*

      I am as raw and bare as one can witness or dare to stare!
Nor do I mince my words either!
Which, like my poor handwriting,
I no longer feel shame in sharing.
No. No, make-up.
I am uneven,
There's no contouring
In these raw wrinkles
Of mine,
That although, still few,
Are no less real than the more-than-few
Sprinkles
Of the pan-cake-powder
I used to put on my face to hide the age
—*or the rage*—
Of having to put on my best face
For having the pressing need to impress.
    Because the foundation
    Of my base was shaky,
Making the connection between my mind and heart
Hazy.
—*Can you feel it — the shift from within?*
    No, I no longer wear make-up!
Because I no longer need a mask
To cover that

I am a mess.
And because I couldn't care less
If you come to love me or
like me any
More
Or —*any less.*
      I do it for myself.
To remove me from the shelf,
And break free from my shell.
No. I. do. Not. Do. Make. Up.
I choose to stand here naked
      With no makeup on my face,
my soul, nor through my pen
Which I use
—*Willingly*—
To break free from all the pain.
Ready to share
And accept
All that I am
And remain
Unrefined and *unfiltered*
      Unafraid
To soak up
The rain
Because
I no longer
Carry— any shame.
      Yet, I am the same,
But
No, I no longer wear make-up;
Because I no longer need to make up
Who I am.

MAKEUP
BEHIND THE LINES:

Makeup came to life in a moment of spontaneity. A family member asked if I had packed makeup for a night out, and without hesitation, I replied, "I don't wear makeup." That simple exchange sparked something deep inside me, and instead of rushing out the door, I rushed to write. The words poured out in their entirety, raw and unfiltered. There's no "makeup" on the writing itself—just like its message, it's honest and true.

The metaphor of makeup in this poem represents the layers we create to meet societal expectations—the masks we wear to fit in or hide parts of ourselves. I've found that when we strip those layers away, we're left with something far more powerful: our authentic selves. The use of terms like *"foundation"* and *"base"* was intentional. A strong, solid foundation within ourselves means we truly know who we are.

Water in this poem symbolizes *renewal* and cleansing, but more importantly, *freedom*—the freedom to stand in the rain and not fear coming undone. But it's not just about makeup being washed away; it's about shedding fear. It's about standing your ground because you know who you are and your true value. This also reflects on my writing—on the way I've learned not to fear expressing my thoughts honestly. *This is me. Unapologetically uncovered.*

I wanted this poem to reflect a world where authenticity is increasingly rare, and to remind anyone reading it that beauty isn't found in filters or masks. It's already within us.

This piece is my way of celebrating the strength that comes from being real, from shedding the layers that don't serve us, and from owning who we are. You don't need to act like anyone or impress anyone. Your superpower lies in you being YOU.

Reader Reflection:

What societal 'foundations' or 'masks' do you rely on to navigate the world, and how might your life change if you embraced your raw, unfiltered truth—without fear of being undone?

Ignliv with YdsLexya

Not ryoneeve anc expereince
the wolrd as you do.

There are people in siht wlord lkie me
taht tannot raed lkie uoy.

Ti sekat me ewtic sa long
ot rdea gniynath
taht nac eb os elpmis
rof srehto.

Take ti morf em:
Ignliv with YdsLexya si drah.

TuB ti si ni eht grit
fo ym luos
I dnfi hte gnertts
ot epoc dna evirht.

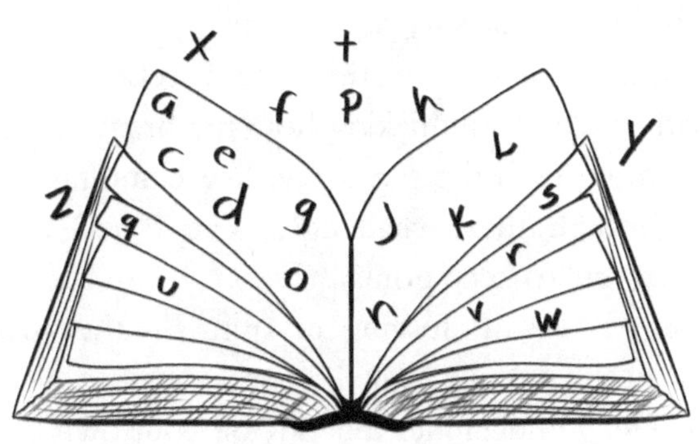

IGNLIV WITH YDSLEXYA
BEHIND THE LINES

Ignliv with YdsLexya captures what it feels like to live with dyslexia. It's not just about the challenge of reading or writing—it's about the frustration, the patience, and the determination it takes to navigate a world that often feels like it wasn't built for me.

Growing up, there wasn't much known about dyslexia. Because I read slowly or had to keep rereading sentences and paragraphs, I was often sent to face the corner of the wall by my professor in front of the entire class. The other kids made fun of me. I developed so many ways to cope, to fit in. Even today, I can't write well by hand—it's often a text only I can decipher.

I didn't let it stop me. Today, I'm a student at the school of my dreams: New York University (NYU). I speak and write fluently in two languages, and I can communicate in Spanish and a little in French. *Don't let anything stop you. Ever.*

The scrambled words in this poem reflect my personal experience with dyslexia, mimicking how my brain processes text. What seems simple for others can feel like climbing a mountain for me. But through these challenges, I've found my grit, my strength, and my will to keep going.

This poem is about thriving in spite of the struggle and finding value in the unique way I experience the world. For a challenge, I will let you decipher this one on your own.

Reader Reflection:

How do you respond to challenges that make you feel different or misunderstood? Have you ever had to develop creative strategies to overcome a struggle that others might take for granted? Reflect on a time when you found strength in what initially felt like a limitation.

Urgency

I write with an urgency
unknown to man.
     Insignificant as I am,
     I write for every woman, man, and child, never able to carry
a pen.
With the *soul* purpose
of *righting* all the wrongs,
that left them without a chance to leave in ink a mark of their
own.
With hope,
 I write to inspire.
Taking pleasure in every consonant and vowel,
binding one to the next in a marriage
forming sounds
     A pleasure they have not yet known.
To defy time, I'll leave behind in ink a mark of my own.
A protest!
A manifesto of a kind
Give every woman, man, and child a pen, I demand!
Let them think and write a story of their own!
Let none go unknown.
I write with urgency.
    Good or bad,
     I write with urgency.
Letting fleets of words meet
with the complete notion that time is limited.

So, when I go,
    I leave behind in ink,
not a life,
but a collection of thoughts worth being known.
Give every woman, man, and child a pen, I demand!
    Let them write a poem of their own!
And God, *please!*
Let no writing go unknown!

URGENCY
BEHIND THE LINES:

Urgency is my manifesto on the transformative power of writing and expression. Writing, to me, isn't just a tool—it's an essential act of existence. It's how we ensure our lives, thoughts, and experiences resonate beyond our physical selves. At its core, this poem *speaks to the Soul purpose of storytelling: the deep human need to share, connect, be understood and hopefully remembered.*

This piece, like most of my writings, came from a personal and passionate place. I wanted to remind myself and others that everyone—regardless of their circumstances—deserves the tools, opportunities, and education to leave their mark. No story should remain untold, no voice unheard. Writing, whether it's in a journal, on a scrap of paper, or in a poem, is how we ensure that our presence lingers in the hearts and minds of others.

The imagery in this poem reflects the intensity of my belief in this call to action, with pens and paper becoming tools of liberation and legacy. The wordplay between *write* and *right* captures my conviction that writing is not only an act of creation but also a way to claim justice and truth. The rhythm and repetition in the poem are purposeful, designed to convey a sense of immediacy, echoing the urgency I feel when words press to escape, demanding to be written.

Urgency isn't just a reflection of my own drive to create; it's a rallying cry for anyone who has ever felt the need to be seen and heard. It's a reminder that your voice matters, your story matters, and you can leave something lasting behind. No one needs to be a wordsmith to write—you just need to write. You should try it. *I recommend it.*

Reader Reflection:

What legacy do you want your words to leave behind? How might expressing your authentic truth help both you and others feel seen, heard, and connected? What is your urgency?

Memories of an Inner Child

I have lived in many houses,
        but never at home.
The plastic bag in which I kept my belongings faithfully aided me
with getting here
and there,
        while facing the unknown.
(How does it feel to have a home?)
I grew up around people but was always left alone.
(How does it feel to never be alone?)

Night after night, my tiny hands clutched the cold metal bars on
the windows, hoping the wind would carry my cries!
        "Mom! Please come home!"
(How does it feel to have a mom?)

Looking out the window, I'd see people going by
        I could not help but wonder which father could be mine.
(What is it like, having a father of your own?)

Do you know what it's like? For a child?
To navigate this world all alone?

I named objects and assigned them life.
In my head, I made them my family in disguise.
(What is it like, having a real one to hold you tight?)

I made my plate with leftovers
As my feet bled, crushed by handed-down, worn-out shoes.
        No one seemed to notice I'd grown.
I slept on the floor because I didn't have a bed of my own
(How does it feel like, to be tucked in after storytime?)
I never had a birthday party, a cake, or a gift to call mine.

(Can someone please describe the feeling of a child blowing out candles and making wishes while others celebrate - THEIR life?!)

I played barefoot with other kids until dark.
I always hoped to be invited in when their parents called them home from the park.
So that, for a moment, I could play pretend
And witness what it's like
To have dinner, not a slice,
    And sit at a table with a mom, a dad, and a sibling who is still alive.

Do you know what it's like? For a child?
To navigate this world alone?

Thank you, *"Mom"*.
Thank you, *"Dad"*.
We shall play this never-ending game again tomorrow
But it's time I went back.
    To the house,
     That will never
     Be a *Home*.

MEMORIES OF AN INNER CHILD
BEHIND THE LINES:

Memories of an Inner Child is deeply personal to me. It reflects the longing, resilience, and pain I experienced growing up without the stability of a traditional family. It touches on universal themes of trauma, child abuse, neglect, and abandonment. Writing this poem felt like a way to give my younger self a voice and to let out the emotions I kept buried for so long. It's my story: growing up not knowing my father, losing my older brother to street violence in Brazil when I was just 12, and watching my mother try her best to raise me despite being so young herself. I've forgiven them both. My father has since passed away, and I now have a great relationship with my mom—something my cancer journey gave me. And then there's Gabriel, my younger brother, who was born on the same date my older brother died but four years later; he brought light and healing into my life.

Back then, it wasn't unusual for kids to be left on their own. My mom and her siblings were, too, and so were my grandparents, great-grandparents and so on. It was a cycle of trauma, passed down and repeated. My mom did the best she could with the weight of her own experiences.

The questions in this poem are raw and direct because they come from the child I was—constantly asking, constantly wondering. They are the kind of questions you don't always get answers to. And when I gave life to objects in the poem, that was my way of showing how I coped as a child. I made those objects my family, my safe space, because I didn't have the real thing. Even the rhythm of the poem mirrors the way I used to think back then—disjointed, searching, trying to make sense of everything around me.

This poem is about belonging—or the lack of it—and how the things we go through as kids don't just disappear when we grow up. If we don't deal with them, they stay with us, shaping who we are. I wanted to connect with anyone who's been through their own unseen battles and remind them that even in the hardest times, we find a way to survive. That resilience can grow into something stronger, and it can lead us toward healing.

If you too went through something like this,
You. Are. Not. Alone.

Reader reflection:

What memories from your childhood still shape the person you are today? What wounds or traumas do you still carry? How might revisiting and embracing your inner child help you find understanding, healing, and strength on your journey?

The Power of Gratitude

Gratitude is Joy.

It encompasses everything,
radiating with the essence of Life.
    A genuine and complete sense of appreciation
    that lights a bright flame,
    emanating from your chest,
    leaving a smile on your face.

Gratitude is Peace—
An overwhelming and quiet sense of contentment
    Like the calming continuous sound of a river flowing
    Or the white noise of waterfalls
    Clearing your mind, inviting stillness to nurture the roots of
your being

It should be practiced as a mantra:
    I am grateful to be alive.
    I am grateful to be healthy.
    I am grateful to and for you.

For your presence—
whether fleeting or lasting,
for the moments we've shared,
and for the ways you've touched my life,
    I am grateful.

I am grateful for the lessons you've taught me,
and for the realization of what truly matters.

I am grateful for the person I am and the person *I am becoming.*
   Gratitude transforms the ordinary into extraordinary.

It is an investment in the Bank of Self-Discovery,
where Love, Empathy, Kindness, Hope, and Compassion
are the currencies that grow the Soul.

So today, and every day,
I carry gratitude in my heart —
letting it guide me,
anchor me,
uplift me,
   and remind me of the gift and power of Now.

THE POWER OF GRATITUDE:
BEHIND THE LINES

I wrote *The Power of Gratitude* on the day my aunt Maria de Lourdes left for London. She had paused her life in Brazil to come to New York and take care of me for nearly five months during one of my many reconstructive surgeries after cancer. During her stay she became one of the biggest supporters of my unapologetic, unfiltered and raw writing style. When she left, the house felt so much emptier, but my heart felt so much fuller. Her love and selflessness reminded me how gratitude can fill the spaces left by life's challenges.

Gratitude has completely changed how I see the world—even how I see struggles. I am even grateful for my cancer. It taught me resilience, gave me a deeper appreciation for life, and revealed strength I didn't know I had. It also helped rebuild a bridge between me and my family, allowing us to reconnect in ways I didn't think were possible. Without it, this book wouldn't even exist. Cancer changed my perspective, helping me find beauty in small details and showing me that every breath is a gift. That's what I wanted this poem to reflect.

In the poem, I use the metaphor of a bank to show how gratitude builds up little by little, like deposits into an account. Those small moments of thankfulness add up to something that can carry you through even the hardest days. I also capitalized words like Gratitude and Soul because, to me, they're so much bigger than just words. They're pillars—foundations that hold me up.

Writing this was my way of honoring not just my aunt, but everyone and everything that's shaped my journey. Gratitude has become my anchor and my compass, guiding me through the highs and the lows. My hope is that this poem reminds anyone reading it that even in the darkest moments, there's always something to be thankful for—and that gratitude has the power to heal.

Reader Reflection:

Think for a moment. How might adopting gratitude as a way of life transform the way you see yourself, your challenges, and the world around you? What are the small moments you can begin to cherish today?

To crack the armor, to lay it bare,
To let the world in, to show we care,
We must surrender, trust and embrace,
The vulnerability of our soul with grace.

MIRRORS AND SHADOWS
Identity and Self-Discovery

Identity: Under You

I,
I fell in between
Silently hidden
Forgotten in the middle.
Pressed in the gaps
Between your snaps
And the cracks of your riddles.

Looking to you for cues
Waiting on clues
So I can shift-shape
Into what you want me to be—
So I don't weigh down your life
With mine.

I stay here silent,
The knot in my throat—hidden,
Forgotten in the middle
Of this emotional mess,
Walking light as air
To avoid cracking the eggs
You so carefully spread.

But I don't know
How much more of this I can take
Before I break—
Splintered, right here, in the middle.

LUCIANA FISHER

Who am I today?
Who do you want me to be?
If it means,
We'll go back to the beginning—
When I
Was enough,
And your words dripped
Nothing but
Sweet, untainted honey
On me.

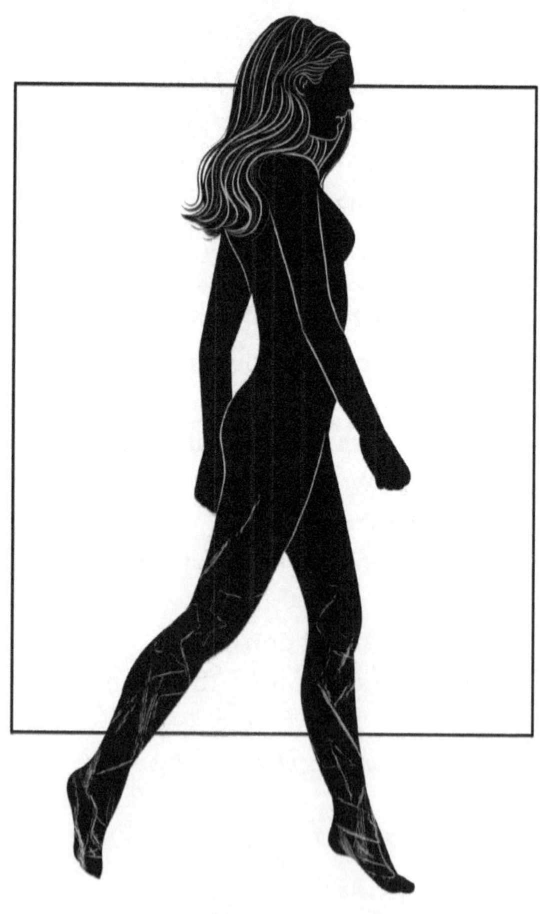

LUCIANA FISHER

IDENTITY: UNDER YOU
BEHIND THE LINES:

Identity: Under You captures what it feels like to lose yourself under the weight of someone else's expectations—especially when their love comes with conditions. Writing this was hard but necessary. It allowed me to finally put into words the quiet sacrifices I made, the resentment that grew in the cracks, and the exhaustion of constantly trying to reshape myself into someone I wasn't.

The metaphor of walking lightly to avoid cracking eggs? That's exactly how it felt. Every move I made had to be calculated to keep the peace, even if it meant losing pieces of myself along the way. The structure of the poem reflects that tension, starting with restraint and eventually breaking down. And then there's the ending—a nod to the love-bombing phase, that first year when everything felt perfect. "Sweet, untainted honey"—I used those words because that's how it felt at first, like pure bliss. But even the sweetest honey eventually leaves a bitter aftertaste when it's layered over control and manipulation.

The questions—Who am I today? Who do you want me to be?—are the thoughts I lived with every day. I was always trying to figure out how to hold on to myself while also trying to be what someone else wanted. Even the pauses in the poem mimic that feeling—like carrying around a weight that never fully leaves.

Writing this helped me make sense of what happened. It showed me just how much I had been forgotten in the middle of it all—lost in the effort to be enough. My hope is that Identity: Under You speaks to anyone who has ever felt diminished or reshaped by a toxic relationship. It's a reminder that you can reclaim who you are, and that real love doesn't ask you to lose yourself.

Reader Reflection:

What parts of yourself have you hidden to keep peace or gain acceptance? How can you begin to honor and reclaim those parts today? Take a moment to reflect: Are you in a relationship that nurtures your authenticity and well-being?

Note to Self

Inside of me and
Never letting me be,
Sticking me in "my place,"
Endless circles in this race.
Curbing my courage,
Undermining my wits,
Restlessly capping my abilities—
Inexplicably,
Trying so hard to fail me, never letting me breathe!

—No, more!

You no longer own me! Step aside, stand down

—Ms. In-se-cu-ri-ty!

NOTE TO SELF
BEHIND THE LINES:

In *Note to Self* I tackle my ongoing battle with insecurity—this relentless voice that constantly tries to hold me back, curbing my courage and undermining my abilities. It's a race that feels endless some days, but writing this poem was my way of pushing back.

By naming and confronting "*Ms. In-se-cu-ri-ty,*" I took back my power. This piece became my declaration of freedom—a true note to self—a reminder that I am more than my doubts and that I can silence that inner critic for good.

This poem was my entry for the first 15-second NPR poetry contest. Even though it had to be short, I wanted it to pack a punch and show the strength it takes to face insecurity head-on. I hope it inspires readers and helps them find the strength to do the same.

Reader Reflection:

What does your inner critic sound like, and how has it tried to hold you back? Think about a time when you pushed back against self-doubt. What did you do to reclaim your power and move forward?

The Paradox of Time

What is time if not an elusive, capricious thing?
We want more of it—but with more of it, we age.
And if we age, we have less time.
What an elusive, capricious thing—time is,

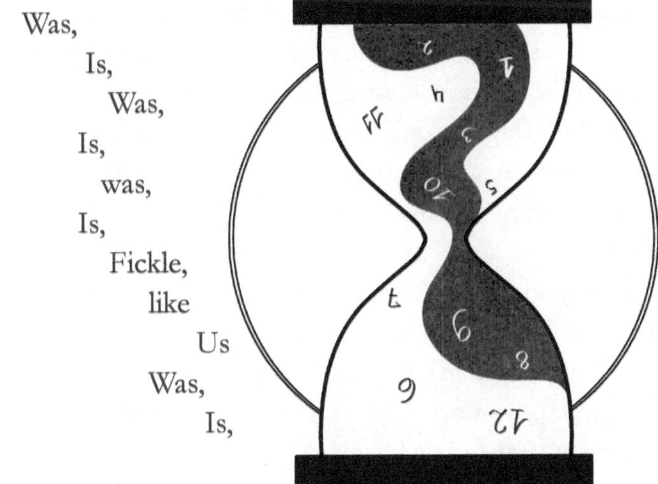

Was,
    Is,
        Was,
    Is,
        was,
    Is,
        Fickle,
            like
                Us
        Was,
            Is,
What an
    Elusive Capricious Thing Time Was—Is—

THE PARADOX OF TIME
BEHIND THE LINES

The Paradox of Time is my reflection on the unpredictable and ever-elusive nature of time. Writing this poem was my way of grappling with its paradox: we crave more time, yet with more time comes aging, and with aging comes less time. It's a loop that feels endless and frustrating but also endlessly fascinating.

The fragmented lines and open-ended structure were intentional, meant to mirror the cyclical and capricious essence of time—how it slips through our fingers while remaining ever-present. The flow of the poem echoes the tic-toc of a clock, capturing the unrelenting passage of moments and the dance between "was" and "is."

This poem isn't about defining time; it's about feeling its contradictions, noticing how it pulls and pushes us, and reflecting on how it shapes our lives.

Time is fickle—just like us—and that's what I wanted to capture here: its ability to feel both fleeting and infinite, merciless and strangely comforting, all at once.

Reader Reflection:

Consider the cyclical nature of time. How do past experiences inform your present, and how might they shape your future?

Who Are We?

Who are we, if not a collection of our memories?
I am the baby on the window,
The girl on the floor,
The teen who could always love more—
Full of hopes and dreams,
The woman who lost a child,
Yet still learned how to sing.

I am a multitude of me(s) and her(s),
Confounded into one:
I am— the one
or was,
Just a second ago;

Now I am already someone new.
For now, I think of things I did not consider minutes before.
Am I still me? Yes. Yet, I am not.

Who are we, if not a collection of our thoughts
And memories?
Do you recall?
I think I remember me—
But who was I then,
When I was the girl on the floor?
I know she wanted more—
I still do, and so does she.
By allowing myself to remember her,
I get to learn more about me.

LUCIANA FISHER

The question remains: who are we,
Without our past lives, selves, and memories?
I remember now. I remember her!
I close my eyes and see her clearly—her, me—
"Hello, little one, come here, child. I've finally found you, the truest form of me!"
By protecting her memory and reigniting her hopes and dreams,
I finally rescued me.

Who Are We?
We are a collection of thoughts and ancestral memories,
Yearning to be set free!

WHO ARE WE?
BEHIND THE LINES:

Who Are We? started as an exploration of identity and memory but turned into a reunion with every version of myself—the baby clutching the window, the girl on the floor, the teen discovering love in all the wrong places, the woman facing loss, and the inner child holding it all together while kicking and screaming to be seen. Writing this poem felt like sitting down with each of them, offering love, acknowledgment, and asking the question: Who am I, really?

This poem reflects how much of who we are today is shaped by the emotions and experiences we carry with us. The imagery—the baby, the girl, the little one—comes from real moments in my life. And the dialogue with the "little one" is deeply personal—it's about finally making room for my inner child, the part of me that has always been there but often went unnoticed.

The repetition and rhythm mirror the process of self-reflection. It's never a straight path—questions lead to more questions, layers are uncovered, and clarity comes in its own time. Writing this felt like piecing together a mosaic of my past selves —some pieces jagged, others smooth, but all of them essential. It reminded me that even the parts of me that once felt lost or broken still hold meaning. Reclaiming them has been a part of finding my way back to myself.

I also wanted to explore a question that has shaped my journey: How do we move forward when the past feels incomplete? Whether it's gaps in memory, unresolved traumas, or simply the way life shapes us, I've learned that healing doesn't mean erasing the past. It means holding it close, reconciling it with the present, and letting it be part of who we are.

This poem is a conversation with myself and the many lives I feel I have lived in my lifetime, but it's also for anyone who has ever felt disconnected from their own story. I hope it inspires you to reconnect with the versions of yourself that still live within you, to honor their resilience, and to find value in every chapter of your journey. We are all made up of our past, present, and the dreams we carry—and every piece belongs. Every piece is part of the puzzle that completes who we are becoming.

Reader Reflection:

Who are you today? How have the hopes, dreams, and challenges of your younger self shaped the person you've become? If you could meet your younger self today, what would you say to them, and how might that conversation guide you toward greater understanding or healing?

Languages

I speak three languages.

The first—
is the language of bossa nova
Where "Rs" rumble in a cadence
born of salt, sand, sea, and samba
Under the open arms
of Christ the Redeemer—

A language twisted and turned
by the broken tongues of the people
taken from their homes
to faraway shores of stolen land.

A colony—
of European and African inheritance,
not weakened,
but enriched by its diversity.
Led by the sole necessity
to sing from its heart.

Unleashing a lyrical powerhouse
to be reckoned with:
        Brazilian Portuguese.

The second—
Is a pragmatic one,
With a complex tense system of verbs,
Relying heavily on word order,
With an even heavier flair for world order.

A rich language
with undeniable global reach,
and vast literary heritage—
Playful, yet direct.

A tongue that everyone and anyone can speak,
Not that it is easy—for it is not.
But it can be diluted,
For and by the deluded,
Who believe by birthright
they have mastered it:
        American English.

But the third?
The third is different.

My most beloved and beautiful—
It is not for the faint of heart.
It is hard and complex.
Few can speak it,
Or write it,
Let alone read it.
Most cannot understand it:
        Poetry.

I speak, read, and write in Portuguese,
—And English.
And somewhere in between,
A meeting of the minds occurs,
Where on most occasions,
it's easy.

I code; you decode.
You code; I decode.
We are done,
Communication happens.

But Poetry?
        Poetry is a lonely language.
I write it, I speak it,
I can read it—
All the lines, around and in between them.
It requires vulnerability,
An open mind and heart
To catch its nuances—
To peel the layers—
But most don't have time to spare.

For the writer,
        Breaking through the fourth wall
Is like finding north without a compass—
        An ancient art,
A science from the days
We traveled by constellations.

A captain without a ship,
Providing a map,
Connecting letters like stars,
        Hoping to lead voyagers
Through the murky waters of metaphors
and symbolisms—
And at times,
A little altercation with *alliteration* —

To find the place
Where all veins meet—the port.

To rest assured
The message—on paper, but not in the bottle—
Arrived safely.
But not everyone can solve the riddle
And reach the shore.

No, poetry is not for the faint of heart.
        I code,
        Who decodes?

Is there anyone out there?

Is there?

        Is there anybody out there?

LANGUAGES
BEHIND THE LINES:

Languages is about the three languages that have shaped me: Portuguese, English, and Poetry. Portuguese was my first; it's where my roots are. It carries the richness of my culture and the complexities of my identity. English came later and took time to feel natural. It became a bridge—a way to access new opportunities and ideas. And then there's Poetry—the language that feels like home. It's not just a way of writing; it's how I connect with the deepest parts of myself.

Writing this poem gave me the space to think about how these languages intersect in my life. Portuguese is intricate; its grammar a bull to master, and we have words that are really hard to translate like "*saudade*." Its beauty reveals itself slowly, requiring patience. English brought a sense of freedom, but it also left parts of me behind, hidden between words. Poetry, though, asks for everything. It's where I feel the most vulnerable and alive.

Speaking more than one language changes you—it changes how you think, how you see the world, even how you express yourself. Poetry does the same for me. It is a magical and an infinite world of possibilities to express your soul artistically and let your imagination run wild and free.

The idea of a "message on paper but not in the bottle" it's

about writing with purpose, knowing there's intention behind every word, even if I don't know who will read it or whether they'll truly understand. It's a vulnerable act, but also a freeing one.

Writing feels like navigating with stars. It's about finding a way through unknown waters, using letters and words as markers to guide the journey. When I write poetry, I am mapping a path through meaning and symbolism, trying to connect with someone who might be looking for the same answers. When I ask, *Is there anyone out there?* It's my own longing for connection. It's the question every writer has—whether their words will matter to someone else.

For me, this poem is about more than languages. It's about the way words connect us, the way they shape who we are, and the hope they carry for being understood.

Reader Reflection:

What language feels most authentic to you—spoken, written, or unspoken? How do the languages you use—through words, actions, or emotions—shape your identity and express your truest self? Who do you hope will decode the messages you send?

Mission

Give yourself permission.

Permission to think,
Permission to rethink,
Permission to talk,
Permission to walk away.

To sit still,
To make noise,
To write and to sing.

To cry and to laugh,
Disrupt, and make peace.

Permission to love,
        to forgive,
To choose,
        to travel.

To feel—
        Eat,
Learn,
        To have an opinion.

To express yourself and make mistakes,
To give up—
        Or start over.

        LUCIANA FISHER

Permission to remember,
        or forget—
To try,
        and fail,
And try again.

Give yourself
permission to be—
Per the mission to live.

MISSION
BEHIND THE LINES:

Mission is an invite, a reminder and call to action all wrapped into one. A reminder to live fully and grant yourself the freedom to be your authentic self and go seek out your dreams. It reflects my own journey toward self-acceptance, where I realized that the permission I was waiting for was already mine to give. Writing it was my way of giving myself the freedom to go after personal growth.

The structure of the poem mirrors its message. The repeated "Permission to…" creates a steady rhythm, inviting readers to pause and reflect. Each line is a small yet meaningful affirmation, touching on everything from stillness to boldness, from trying and failing to starting again—permission to write, for example, means to share my writings, my thoughts, to read and perform my works live on stage. It's about not caring what others will think and being unapologetically myself.

It took a four-year cancer battle to get me here. But I am here. And I hope to connect genuinely with readers, to engage, to meet, and to continue doing live readings and performances— maybe one day even beyond the confines of my state borders to read.

The closing lines, "Permission to be— / Per the mission to live," hold the heart of the poem. They remind us that living is both an intentional act and a courageous one, requiring self-compassion and the willingness to accept our own humanity. I hope to inspire others to live boldly, to go of external validation. Life is so short! Facing mortality taught me to let go and let live.

Reader Reflection:

What permissions have you been waiting for in life? How might granting yourself the freedom to think, feel, and take risks help you live more authentically and fully?

When we open the chambers of our heart,
When we allow it to play its part,
We invite others to do the same,
To share their stories without shame.

THE THREADS THAT BIND US
Relationships and Connection

Tend to What Matters

Friendships and relationships,
Like flowers and plants,
Will wilt without care.

We're all in charge of watering,
Of letting the light in.

Look for the warning signs—
Drooping leaves,
Fading petals.

When you see them,
Take the time to:
Recut the stems,
Warm the water,
Sprinkle some sugar.

And watch—
When nurtured,
How they grow.

TEND TO WHAT MATTERS
BEHIND THE LINES:

Tend to What Matters is a simple yet powerful reminder that relationships, like plants, need care, attention, and intention to thrive. I wrote this poem thinking about the friendships and connections that have shaped my life—the ones that flourished because they were nurtured and the ones that withered due to neglect.

I know the theme here is not new, but I hope my take is. Relationships, like anything living, are not self-sustaining. They require effort, presence, and an awareness of the small signs that something needs tending. It's easy to assume that love, trust, and connection will always be there, but like flowers without water, they fade if left unattended. The imagery of drooping leaves and fading petals serves as a metaphor for the subtle signs of distance, exhaustion, or unspoken needs between people.

The small gestures—recutting the stems, warming the water, adding sugar—symbolize the care we put into maintaining these bonds. Sometimes, it's as simple as checking in, listening, or making space for someone when they need it most.

At its core, this poem is a call to mindfulness in our relationships. Just as a plant perks up with a little care, so too can a relationship when given love, presence, and attention. If something is important to you, tend to it.

Reader Reflection:

Think about the relationships in your life—friendships, family, love. Are there any that need watering? Are there subtle signs that you've overlooked? How can you take small, intentional steps today to nurture the connections that matter most?

What Was Left Unsaid

This could have been a love story—
of us!
Granddaughter and grandmother
Both fragile, strong—and stubborn—
We allowed resentment to build up in the cracks, and
longing to linger in the seams.

As the years passed—
We danced around the silence for far too long.

I wanted you to see me.
Not the version you wanted me to be,
but me.
Did you ever?

I wanted to let go—
of the chains of your expectations,
the weight of my anger.
I wanted to love you.
I wanted you to love me,
freely.

But the words caught in my throat.
I never said them.
You never said them.

Did we leave it unsaid—
or worse,
did we fail to feel it at all?

     LUCIANA FISHER

This could have been a love tale.
But *we failed* to lay the bricks
that could have built us.
And now—
Time has run out.
The chance is gone.

Rest in peace, Grandma.
I *loved* you.

WHAT WAS LEFT UNSAID
BEHIND THE LINES:

What Was Left Unsaid reflects the complexities of love, regret, and the unspoken dynamics within family relationships. It was inspired by my complicated relationship with my grandmother— a bond that was strained and distant, marked by silence and tensions. The poem captures the fragile line between longing and resentment, the weight of unmet expectations, and the pain of missed chances for us to build a real connection.

Writing it was my way of facing the regret I feel over the things I never said. I still wonder if she felt the same. The image of "laying bricks" represents the emotional work needed to build meaningful relationships—a work we never did. Instead, silence defined our relationship, and in the end, that silence became the wall between us.

The structure mirrors the unresolved nature of our bond, with unanswered questions and emotions left hanging. The ending, a final goodbye, is both an apology and my attempt at closure. It's my way of saying I cared, even if I couldn't express it the way I wanted to.

This poem isn't just a reflection—it's a reminder of how important it is to say what needs to be said while we still can. I hope it encourages readers to think about their own relationships and the words they may still have time to say.

Reader Reflection:

What words have you left unsaid in your relationships? How might expressing them now—while there's still time—change the connection you share with your loved ones?

What Love Is

You will not know what love is
When chemistry floods your brain,
When butterflies fly in your belly,
When they know exactly how to pull you closer—
Fingers tracing the back of your neck,
Through your hair,
Bringing your lips to theirs.
So close you can feel their soft, sweet breath
Entering your body,
As if their soul is merging with yours,
And yours with theirs.
When a jolt of electricity runs through you,
Delivering you to burning desire,
Raising the temperature in the room,
Lighting fireworks within you,
Dropping you to your knees,
Leaving you begging, *please.*

You will not know they are the one.
You will not know what love is.
You will know what passionate lust is.

But love is different.

You will know they are the one
When you feel safe,
When your needs are met,
When they support your dreams.

     LUCIANA FISHER

When their presence brings calm and comfort,
And your trust stays unbroken.
When discussions lead to growth,
And apologies are heartfelt, sincere.
When your agency is not taken away,
And your freedom is not a threat but encouraged.
When they make life a little less heavy,
A bit more colorful.
When they see the beauty of your soul,
Admire the depth of your thoughts,
And are captivated by the brilliance of your mind.

And finally, you will know...

Not in
the rush,
the spark,
the fire.
Not when your head is in the clouds,
But when your feet are firmly anchored on the ground.

You'll feel it in the calm,
When love simmers slow and steady—
Its hum gentle, its noise low.

WHAT IS LOVE
BEHIND THE LINES:

This poem was inspired by a conversation with my brother Gabriel during one of our afternoon walks to grab lunch at a local restaurant. We talked about life, love, and how the possibility for true love only reveals itself after the initial infatuation fades. The fiery sparks, the butterflies, and the overwhelming passion are thrilling, but they're not the whole story. That kind of love— the chemical rush—is what Hollywood and the media condition us to crave. It's an addiction, really, and it isn't realistic.

Real love, as we saw it, exists in the calm that follows. It's in the moments when the intensity cools and there's space to decide if a connection will deepen and grow or fade and disappear. Writing this poem was my way of reflecting on that conversation and exploring what happens in that in-between space. It's about realizing that love isn't about being swept off your feet but about finding solid ground with someone who makes life lighter, brighter, and worth sharing.

The poem contrasts the fleeting allure of lust with the steady, grounding connection of lasting love—love built on trust, respect, and showing up for each other. It's a reflection on what it truly means to find "the one" and what love, at its core, really is.

I dedicate this poem to Gabriel, who inspired this reflection, and to anyone searching for or holding onto this kind of love. It's a reminder that true connection doesn't live in the rush but in the quiet moments that follow. If you're looking for real connection and enduring love, be careful not to fall too deeply into the trappings of chemical love. True connection grows not in the rush but in the calm.

Reader Reflection:

In your life, have you ever mistaken passionate lust for enduring love? Did you believe at the time they were "the one"? What has that experience taught you about what love truly is

Connection

I want to dive,
swim —
in the wet, warm darkness
of the light emanating
from the iris of your eyes.

To be imprinted in the retina,
expanding the pupils
to black hole proportions,
its gravity sucking me
into the universe of your *mind*.

To witness what it's like
to experience life
beneath these skies—
    through the eclipse
    of your sight.

CONNECTION
BEHIND THE LINES:

This poem was born from a moment—one of those fleeting, magnetic encounters where you feel completely drawn into someone's soul. It's about longing not just to see, but to truly understand, to inhabit someone's experience, even if just for a moment.

I was captivated by the way eyes communicate and tell stories. How they reflect light yet conceal darkness—how they can pull you in like gravity, like black holes swallowing everything in their wake. There's something almost cosmic about the depth of another person's gaze, the way it can transport you, make you question what it really means to "see" someone.

The line *"through the eclipse of your sight"* is central to the poem's meaning. It's not just about vision—it's about perspective, about understanding someone from the inside out. The eclipse is both a barrier and an invitation—what happens when we step into the unknown, into another's darkness?

This isn't just a poem about sight, but about immersion, about connection beyond words. About having the ability to dive into their inner world. It's about being pulled into someone's world so completely that, for a moment, your reality bends to theirs.

Unfortunately, we can never fully, truly know someone, can we?

Reader Reflection:

Have you ever felt completely drawn into someone's world —where a single glance, a moment, or a conversation made you feel like you understood them beyond words—or wanted to?

Stitch

I could stare at you all day,
As you meet my gaze and rarely look away
I remember the first time I saw you,
So tiny! You could fit in the palm of my hand.

You were always shy and afraid,
Hiding under every piece of furniture,
As I begged, *Come out, and play.*
It took you some time,
But one day, you came out from under the table,
And never looked back, ready to turn my life upside down in the
best possible way.

Now, far from shy,
I hear the clicking sound as you make your rounds,
Head up high, fiercely confident.
You own this house,
        You protect me and keep me company.

As you bark your way,
With energy unmatched
You fill this house with life and so much joy,
Always ready to play,
My miniature black dot,
        I will always keep you safe,
As you schnauzer about your day.

    LUCIANA FISHER

STITCH
BEHIND THE LINES:

Stitch is my tribute to my miniature black Schnauzer, who has brought so much joy and love into my life. Writing this poem was my way of expressing just how grateful I am for the bond we share and the impact he has had on my world. I remember when he was timid, hiding under tables and furniture, and now he's a confident, headstrong companion who has been my constant source of comfort, connection, and happiness.

I wrote this poem (one of many he has inspired me to write), to capture the little moments that make our relationship so special—the clicking of his paws as he makes his rounds, the way he claimed his space in my home and in my heart, and the endless joy he brings to my life. Stitch came into my life at a time when I needed light and healing, and he has been a daily reminder of the unconditional love that makes life brighter.

This poem is about the love we find in those who see us completely and love us unconditionally. Through this poem, I honor Stitch and all the ways he has brought healing and happiness into my life.

Spidey

You are always there,
Here, and everywhere!
Trailing behind with your sweet temper,
Always calm—while you follow me around.

It's been eleven years,
Of you making my favorite sound—
A tiny puppy's high-pitched howl,
Sounding like: *youyouyouyou!*

My sweet boy,
    Grab that toy!
     Let *me* follow you around,
As you go about wagging your tail
     And filling my world with my forever favorite sound!

 LUCIANA FISHER

SPIDEY
BEHIND THE LINES:

Spidey is my joyful tribute to my Yorkie, Spidey, who has been my loyal companion for over a decade. Writing this poem was my way of celebrating the simple, heartwarming moments that define our bond—his playful energy, his unique high-pitched "youyouyouuu" sound, and the way his wagging tail lights up my world. Spidey has been my constant shadow, always by my side with his gentle temperament and quirky personality.

This poem captures the beauty of companionship, and the happiness found in life's smallest moments. Spidey has taught me to appreciate the irreplaceable joy of unconditional love—the kind that makes even the most ordinary days brighter. Writing this was a reminder for me to treasure every sound, every wag, and every playful moment because they are what make our connection so special.

Through this poem, I want to celebrate not just my bond with Spidey but the profound connection we share with our pets, who bring so much love and meaning into our lives.

Reader Reflection:

Think about the pets who have shared your life—what have they taught you about love, joy, and companionship? How do their unique quirks and unconditional presence bring meaning to your everyday moments?

We christen a child when it's born
and shower it with love out of **nothing**
As the child grows, we teach it to pursue
nothing but what has the value of **gold**
We rob them of their innocence and dreams
by telling them what they **can**
Or cannot achieve measured by our wooden spoon
of failures, and all that cannot **stay**

Dreams Should Stay.

golden shovel

INK, FIRE, AND REBELLION
Creativity and Expression

A Poem Waiting to Be Born

There is a poem in me—
I must birth it to set it free.

At this moment, I cannot write.
    I have been stripped of a power I'm not even sure I ever
had.
Inspiration has ceased to inspire.
The muse has left the building without notice.
Luck did not show its face, did not meet me with grace.
    The words do not flow, do not pour out,
though I have a burning message within,
pressing to fill the pages, overpowering their blank state.

But no—
no inspiration, no flow, no show.
It's been 21 days, but it feels like 9 months.
Can someone, anyone, turn on the faucet,
open the waterfall of words, drench me in its river—
let even the bacteria in my gut bask in its liquid joy,
like food feeding the brain, like water absorbed by the soul,
quenching a thirst for words that carry meaning,
that convey the message I cannot hold back.

Words I have buried so deep.
They lie inside, restless,
like a fetus punching, pushing, and pulling,
waiting to be born, to be freed.
I beg you—be expelled, be seen, be read, be free!

Inspiration lingers, spies on me.
It is here, in this room, hiding, laughing, mocking me—
A volatile Goddess!
Daring me to write something, anything,
without first bending the knee.

The message, like a wildfire burning coal,
like a diamond in the rough,
waiting to be honed, crafted, shaped—
let the world in, let the words out.
Let every pore breathe out the message pounding from within.

There is a universe of words inside every vowel,
a madness of consonants in my head, forming sounds.
Evil witch—help me. There is a poem in me! — I scream.
Pull it out. Even if dragged by its hair.
How unfair!

I bend the knee, *Inspiration*, I beg of thee—
There is a poem in me.
I must birth it out—
to be free.
Come to me.
Be the midwife, *I beg of thee.*

A POEM WAITING TO BE BORN
BEHIND THE LINES:

A Poem Waiting to Be Born is my dramatic reflection on the creative struggle and the feeling of powerlessness when the words just won't come. This poem is, yet again, deeply personal to me. After my uncle passed away, I couldn't write for 21 days. The grief and emotional weight left me completely disconnected from my ability to express myself—a frustration that felt stifling and impossible to escape. Writing this piece was my way of processing that silence and the urgency I felt to let the words out.

The imagery of buried words, a restless fetus, and inspiration as a mocking, capricious force captures the tension I felt between the desire to create and the inability to do so. I wanted to reflect the raw vulnerability of that moment—the yearning to give birth to something meaningful and the helplessness of being unable to make it happen. Inspiration, personified as a volatile goddess, became my way of grappling with grief and the unpredictable nature of creativity.

This poem wasn't just about my frustration it was a plea for release writing allowed me to confront my grief and begin to reconnect with the very act of writing. It's a testament to the resilience of creativity, even when it feels buried under loss and exhaustion, and a reminder that creating is as much about the struggle as it is about the inspiration.

Rest in Peace, Uncle Robson.

Reader Reflection:

Have you ever experienced a time when grief or emotional weight silenced your voice or creativity? How can allowing yourself patience and compassion help you find your way back to expression?

A Poem Waiting to Be Found

There is a poem here,
but I don't want to promote it.

I don't want it to come to you — *that easily.*
I want you to come to it.
To find it.
To rescue it from a strange corner on the internet,
from a dusty shelf,
or a quiet store.

I want it to find a home in your home,
to travel with you in your car,
to be tucked in your purse.
I want your eyes to see it,
and your heart to feel it.
For you to treasure it,
because it brings meaning to a moment,
or revives a memory.

And in the process,
I want it to rescue you.

I want you to find it in the corner café,
in the hands of a beautiful stranger,
so captivated, they miss your gaze.
To find it in the book your best friend swears you'll love.

I want it to surprise you,
to stop you mid-scroll.

To be among the pages you turn
with careful fingertips,
you've press to your lips.

I want you to read it on a subway car in a strange country,
on your commute to work,
in the back of a car on a mid-summer ride,
with your windows down,
feeling the breeze and the warmth of the sun on your skin.
I want you to remember it.

I want it to consume you, to inspire you.
For you to give it meaning—
draw from it what you need,
whatever it serves.

I want you to rescue my poetry from its solitude.
I want it to give you pause.
To keep you company,
and to be the company you keep.

To be found by chance,
and kept by choice.

I don't want to promote my poetry,
but quietly, I hope it finds the world.
I want it to speak volumes,
to find you when it's ready—
to slip into your heart
and add poetry to your life.

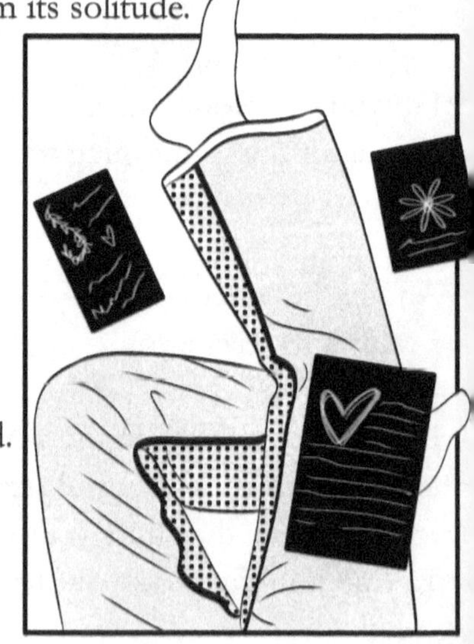

     LUCIANA FISHER

A POEM WAITING TO BE FOUND
BEHIND THE LINES:

A Poem Waiting to Be Found reflects what could be the dream of every creator. It is my quiet hope that my poetry will connect with readers in unexpected and meaningful ways. Writing this piece was my way of imagining the journey my words might take —the hands they might land in and the lives they might touch.

After reading the poem, a fellow writer shared this reflection with me: *"To be able to express what every poet feels is a rare talent. To do it so well and so vividly, rarer still. I reread this several times and I stopped mid-scroll in a different place each time. This is so good! 'To be found by chance and kept by choice' is brilliant!"* Their words captured exactly what I was trying to convey: the hopes and dreams poets and writers carry, that our work will gain a life of its own in the hands of readers, maybe even across the world.

This poem is a love letter to that dream and to the serendipity of connection—those unexpected moments when words find their way to someone who truly needs them. It's not about recognition or fame, but about trust: trusting that the right words will find the right reader at the right time.

So, if you are reading this poem, if it reached you, or touched you, in any way. I hope you write to me and let me know how far it has traveled in this world.

I cannot wait to know who you are.

Reader Reflection:

Have you ever discovered something unexpected that deeply resonated with you? How might allowing space for serendipity in your life open the door to moments of connection and inspiration?

Expectations

Sad realization —
our writing is not always going to be good,
just as our food is not always going to be good.

At least, maybe not to your palate. Or theirs. His or hers.
Sometimes, not even mine.

Perfection will not be achieved on a daily basis. Period.

Even sex is not always going to be good.

Ground your expectations.

Like cooking or any art form, writing is a process.
        Sometimes we burn the chicken, oversalt the fish,
        over-season the meatloaf, devour each other
        too hard, too slow—
write too little, or too much—
and say too much, or nothing at all.

Perfection will not be achieved on a daily basis. Period.
Ground your expectations.

The spices of my food and of my words
will not always be dosed just right
for you, or in the exact measure that pleases everyone.

We will not always. Please. Everyone.

But there is one person you can please:
yourself.
      If you try, and don't give up,
       you will only strengthen yourself.

Cook, if that is your passion.
Or rearrange the photos on the wall,
the furniture on the ground.
Paint that canvas hidden in the corner.
Pick up the pencil and draw on the subway,
take the pen and write first thing in the morning
or late in the evening.

Write when inspiration visits unexpectedly
and a masterpiece can be born—
      but also write when it doesn't,
       and a poem as ordinary as this lands on the page.

Make art when energy in motion *flows* through you,
like the blood in your veins,
the speed of your heartbeat,
the tear rolling down your face,
the laughter you cannot contain.

Express your soul. The outcome is the art.

And sometimes, in rare moments,
the trinity aligns, the universe says yes,
and the pearly gates of heaven,
guarded by the gods of Art,
opens so they can grace us with their presence.

After much experimentation, patience, and acceptance—
the magic happens.
The real masterpiece is the process:
The art of connecting with yourself.
Find joy in the process of self-expression,
and once you've connected, *let your soul aim for the stars.*

EXPECTATIONS
BEHIND THE LINES:

Expectations is my reflection on the creative process and the unrealistic standards I often impose on myself. I wrote this poem as a personal reminder to let go of perfectionism and to appreciate the messy, beautiful journey of creating. It captures my struggles with self-doubt and the pressure to constantly produce something exceptional, using everyday metaphors like cooking to show the unpredictable nature of inspiration.

The repetition of "Perfection will not be achieved on a daily basis. Period." became my grounding mantra while writing this piece—a reminder that imperfection isn't just inevitable, it's essential. Writing, like cooking, is full of trial and error, burnt chicken, over-seasoned meatloaf, or a poem that doesn't quite land. But it's through these missteps that growth and authenticity emerge (and we develop our skills!).

For me, the real masterpiece isn't the final product—it's the act of connecting with myself through self-expression. I'm writing, painting, rearranging photos, or laughing uncontrollably, I've learned that art happens in those fleeting moments when energy in motion flows through us. Expectations is my way of reminding myself to find joy in those moments and to keep creating, even when the outcome isn't perfect.

I hope this poem encourages readers to let go of perfection, honor the creative process, and find the courage to keep going. The magic isn't in getting it perfect—it's in daring to express yourself and aiming for the stars.

Reader Reflection:

What expectations have you placed on yourself in your creative or everyday pursuits? Have you ever felt the weight of expectations others project onto you? How might releasing these pressures allow you to find greater joy, authenticity, and freedom in your self-expression?

Uncomfortable

I am uncomfortable
With the way you *lie*,
Uncomfortable with the way you procrastinate on your life
As if tomorrow is promised.

I am uncomfortable watching you comfortably rot,
Wasting every second of your existence,
Like sand slipping through your fingers,
Chasing nothing but the next fix of air to breathe.

I am uncomfortable watching you not read,
Write, or create anything.
Uncomfortable listening to the excuses you give
For all the things you will never make,
Wishing while you lie awake,
Telling yourself all the things you will never do.

I am uncomfortable.
Being you—
When we could be so much more,
If only you would take the first step
And begin to do something—for you.

UNCOMFORTABLE
BEHIND THE LINES:

This poem is about frustration. It's a confrontation, an unraveling of a truth most don't always want to admit: that we can be complicit in our own stagnation, that the comfort of avoidance is its own quiet destruction. But is this a callout or a self-reckoning? A warning or a confession?

The word *lie* holds everything together, twisting between meanings — deception, stillness, avoidance, self-sabotage. Do we lie to ourselves first, convincing ourselves there's still time, that we'll start tomorrow? Or is it our inaction, our willingness to *lie still*, that gives birth to the deception? And if both are true, where does the cycle break?

This poem moves in an inescapable cycle where no one — speaker, listener, or reader — is free from the paradox. The I calls out the *you*, but are they separate, or simply two versions of the same self? The reader steps into the confrontation, unknowingly becoming part of it. The poem doesn't offer an escape—just a mirror, reflecting the uncomfortable truth back at whoever dares to look.

Reader Reflection:

Where do you see yourself in this poem? Are you the reader, the speaker or the listener? Are you the one who calls out, or the one being called out? Or both?

Pickle

To tickle my creativity pickle,
I self-prescribed a dose of writing — once a day.
— *ONCE* —
Therefore, this is my writing for today.

PICKLE
BEHIND THE LINES:

Pickle is my playful take on the process of writing and the discipline it takes to keep going. I wrote this poem during a moment when I needed to honor my commitment to writing daily—a self-prescribed dose of creativity. It reflects how creativity can show up in unexpected, quirky forms and reminds me that sometimes just showing up to write is more important than the result.

With its humor and simplicity, this poem captures the idea that not everything I or anyone writes has to be profound or polished all the time. We can let go and have fun! For me, *Pickle* is a lighthearted nod to the persistence, humor, and small victories that keep me moving forward on this creative journey.

Reader Reflection:

How do you find humor or lightness in moments of frustration or creative block?

Modern Life

I had no expectations,
But—My Lord!
This soup is exquisite!
My, oh my!
I can tell you—my belly is full. Bulging.
I'm stuffed.

—Waiter! (finger snap!)
What's the special? I'm on a gluten-free diet.
And I'll have another, if you please!

—Absolutely, Sir! Right away!
Another bowl of Simple Life Soup du Jour is coming right up!

—Sir—We have Happiness on a Platter, a crowd favorite!
And for dessert, may I suggest a Mousse of Joy?
Light as air, with a delicate dash of laughter on top!
Don't worry; it's all allergen-free!

—Great! I'll have that!
And to drink—what are they having over there?

—The couple over there, Sir? They're sipping Love on Tap.

—Great, I'll have that now. Fill my cup and keep it coming,
please!

—Would you also care for a bit of Sadness Tea with your Joy, Sir?

—Well, why not?! Bring it!
I'm sure I can handle it!

—Right away, Sir! A perfect choice.
After all, there's always room for more, is there not?
How about our exclusive serving of Regret?

—Regret? Hmm—Oh, Boy! Exclusive?!?! HOW EXCITING!!!

—Indeed, Sir. Our Regret is hand-crafted and aged to perfection
—an absolute rarity! A delicacy that lingers long after the first
taste.

MODERN LIFE
BEHIND THE LINES:

Modern Life is my playful yet biting commentary on the absurdities of modern consumer culture. Writing this poem gave me the chance to explore themes like gluttony, greed, superficiality, and regret, reflecting on how life often feels like an elaborate menu of choices—some fulfilling, others hollow. By presenting emotions and experiences as consumable items, I wanted to show how we package and indulge in these offerings without stopping to question their real value.

The humor and irony throughout the poem allowed me to critique the endless pursuit of fulfillment. Exaggerated dishes like "Happiness on a Platter" and "Regret, aged to perfection" were designed to provoke both laughter and reflection. Through this, I am asking: *Are we savoring life, or just stuffing ourselves with whatever is marketed to us?*

I originally wrote this poem for a competition that required using the word soup or souper, but I missed the deadline to submit it. Even though I couldn't enter, I'm still proud of how it turned out. This poem invites readers to think about the metaphorical "menu" they order from in their own lives and whether their choices truly nourish their souls.

For me, this poem is a reminder to be mindful of what we consume—not just physically, but emotionally and spiritually—and to recognize the difference between indulging in life and truly living it.

Reader Reflection:

What does your personal 'menu' of life look like? Are you savoring meaningful experiences, or are you chasing temporary satisfaction? How could you make more mindful choices about what truly nourishes your soul?

Virtuality

What can I *caption*
that you have not seen or heard?
In the era we are the herd.
Followed, unfollowed, and blurred.
Swiping unsure of who we are or were.
Where a tick that is *blue*
Only turns us blue
With envy and sorrow
While our mental health sees no tomorrow
Only instant grams of falsehoods and scams,
Where we wear a filter but have no filter.
Where hate only grows, and love seldom shows—
Yet in an instant reel, we waste another minute.
To conceal our pain, we swipe again,
While we go insane
For likes often filled with disdain!
And yet we swipe again,
Left and right,
With no end in sight.
But a voice inside says, *Set the phonies aside*
And stand beside
Your best friend, Pride;
And unfriend the *friend*
That knows your name
But not your pain,
Online
For a matter of gain,

Sharing endlessly in vain
For an instant claim
To fame.
Set the device aside,
Reconnect with your pride.
If you're in it for the ride,
Self-esteem is the prize.

     LUCIANA FISHER

VIRTUALITY
BEHIND THE LINES:

Virtuality reflects my frustrations with living in a hyper-connected but isolating digital world. Writing this poem was my way of dealing with the struggle between craving online validation and wanting real, unfiltered authenticity. It's so easy to get lost in the endless scroll, chasing likes and approval while neglecting what truly matters—genuine connection.

This poem was inspired by the moment social media platforms started selling blue verification ticks. What was once a symbol of credibility become just another thing people could buy, another commodity! Watching how quickly people became consumed with this need for validation, alongside the toxic environments online, the extreme use of filters, and the influencer gold rush, made me stop and think. *How can we be more connected than ever but still feel so alone?*

Lines like *"Where we wear a filter but have no filter"* and *"Sharing endlessly in vain for an instant claim to fame"* reflect what I see as the erosion of self-esteem and the constant pressure to conform to digital ideals. For me, this poem became a reminder to set my device aside, reconnect with who I really am, and focus on the relationships that matter the most.

At its core, *Virtuality* is about reclaiming self-worth, authenticity, and meaningful connection over the fleeting rewards of the digital world. I hope it encourages readers to take a step back, reflect, and focus on what really nourishes their souls.

Reader Reflection:

In our hyper-connected digital world, have you ever felt disconnected from yourself or others? What steps might you take to reclaim your sense of authenticity and focus on meaningful connections? How can you prioritize self-worth over fleeting online validation?

It takes courage to be truly known,
To let your heart's melody in the fold.

WHEN ABSENCE SPEAKS
Loss, Grief, and Legacy

Breathe

Inhale—
    Exhale.
Aspire—
    To inspire.
Inhale—
    Exhale.

The Absence of You

The wind is blowing.
There is snow on the ground now.
The cold is fitting.
I welcome it, yet it feels even colder inside — *where I cannot find the warmth — of you.*
Time did not get the memo, as though it refuses to acknowledge
the weight of this moment—
the stillness that should accompany such loss.
First day of winter, I was told.
No wonder there is snow on the ground.

The trees are now bare
As I sit here and stare
At tiny cars and buses
With little people in them go by.

Doing. Going. Turning. Existing.
Moving without pause, while I remain here, anchored by loss.

Did they not get the memo?
Where are they going?
What are they doing?
Living their lives unaware that Earth is standing still?

That we should all stop and let out a collective cry so loud
It would be nothing short of a deafening sound.

Are they not aware?
That ocean levels should rise and swell with the weight of

collective grief,
tides should crash as though the earth itself weeps —
a tsunami, a hurricane —
Earth itself mourning the absence of you?

But the world goes on,
As if it was not swallowed whole
By the black hole created when your *light went out.*

They did not get the memo.
They move unaware that the universe reached inside my chest
And ripped my heart out.
They go about their day, travelling in their toy buses and cars.

But the world moves on,
Unaware of the memo it never received. *Unaware* that is moving
on without you.

The snow will end, melting quietly into the ground as it does
every season —
a soft surrender to the inevitable march of time —
as it goes only forward, indifferent to the weight of my sorrow.
It will continue to refuse to stop.
The next season will come, and the next.

The oceans will not rise, for my tears will go dry.
The pain will subside, in equal measure that the longing will grow.

And only I will know the depth of what the world has lost —
someone as wonderful as you.

THE ABSENCE OF YOU
BEHIND THE LINES:

The Absence of You is my reflection on loss and grief, written as an attempt to step into the shoes of my friend J., who lost their partner a few years ago. One afternoon, just before Christmas 2024, I sat at my computer working on my poetry while watching the relentless pace of the world—cars, buses, and people going about their lives. I thought of J. and their loss, imagining how the holiday season might amplify their pain.

In a moment of synchronicity, I received a text from J. right then: "Holiday time is always a little hard. Grief is the worst this time of the year but managing through it as best as I can." That message became the spark for this poem—a way to honor J.'s grief and the quiet, isolating weight of absence during a season that so often revolves around togetherness.

The imagery of changing seasons, melting snow, and the indifference of time reflects how life inevitably moves forward, even when grief keeps us anchored in place. Lines like "Did they not get the memo?" and "The universe reached inside my chest and ripped my heart out" capture the dissonance between internal mourning and the external world, which doesn't pause for anyone's pain.

I wrote this poem to connect with others who feel this dissonance—to offer a mirror to their grief and a reminder that they are not alone.

I dedicate this poem to you, J.

Reader Reflection:

Have you ever paused to consider the unseen pain others may be carrying on any given day? How might cultivating empathy for their struggles deepen your connection to the world around you? What pain are you carrying in isolation? How might acknowledging and sharing it bring you closer to healing or connection with others?

The Meaning of Goodbye

Goodbye is growth.

There comes a moment when you will do something for the last time. Maybe you'll realize it, maybe you won't. But in that moment, a shift will occur. Your compass will point in a new direction. Your frequency will change, recalibrating the course of your life.

If you allow it,
if you commit to authenticity,
you'll recognize that it no longer serves you.

And then you jolt.

It feels like being swept into a tidal wave. A surge of self-awareness crashes over you, leaving you both exhilarated and terrified. Clarity floods your mind.

"This is finished," you realize.
"It no longer serves me. It no longer aligns with the person I am becoming."

It's bittersweet. Nostalgic. Exciting. Scary.

The emotions move through your body in waves—
from your mind to your toes,
settling finally in your heart.

You feel gratitude for the lessons, the memories, the laughter. But it's time to move forward. Some people, some places, will remain part of your journey. Others will fade, becoming footnotes in the story of your life.

When the time comes,
Honor it. Be present.

True transformation only happens when you fully acknowledge it. Without awareness, the moment will pass, and you'll find yourself stuck in the same place, repeating the same patterns.

There may be false starts—moments when you thought you were ready but weren't. Forgive yourself for those times. They were preludes, trials, the necessary groundwork for what is to come.

When the right moment arrives,
you'll know.

You are transforming.

The chrysalis is breaking open.

Fly, butterfly.

Say goodbye, not with fear, but with love.
And step into your truest self.

Go experience new things.
And remember you are deeply loved,
and never alone.

Say goodbye. Go, and grow!

THE MEANING OF GOODBYE
BEHIND THE LINES:

The Meaning of Goodbye is my attempt to make sense of the emotional complexities of saying goodbye. For me, goodbyes have always carried weight—fear, hope, nostalgia, curiosity, anxiety, and the bittersweet anticipation of what's next. Writing this poem was my way of exploring the power of letting go, not as an ending but as a step toward growth. It's a reminder that transformation often begins where comfort ends.

I wrote this piece in Miami on the day I was heading back to New York after Art Basel. In that moment, I realized I needed to say goodbye to a lifestyle that no longer fit the person I am growing into. The butterfly theme came to me while staring at the wallpaper in one of the bathrooms at my dear friend R.'s home. I was fixing my hair, and in the reflection of the mirror, I could see the butterfly wings behind me. My imagination ran wild, as if I were wearing their wings. It was a quiet, insightful moment that gave me pause, and suddenly, the symbolism of the chrysalis breaking open became the heart of the poem.

Goodbyes often show up at key moments, urging us to recalibrate and move forward. This poem captures the emotions tied to those transitions—gratitude for what has been, fear of the unknown, and the courage it takes to step into something new. Lines like "It no longer serves me. It no longer aligns with the person I am becoming" reflect the clarity that comes from deep reflection and the bravery it takes to honor that clarity.

I hope this poem inspires readers to see goodbyes not as something to fear but as opportunities to step into who they are meant to be. It's about breaking free from the chrysalis and trusting yourself to take flight.

Reader Reflection:

What aspects of your life no longer serve the person you are becoming? How might accepting change and finding the courage to say goodbye, open the door to your transformation? Are you ready to take a leap of faith and take flight or do you fear it?

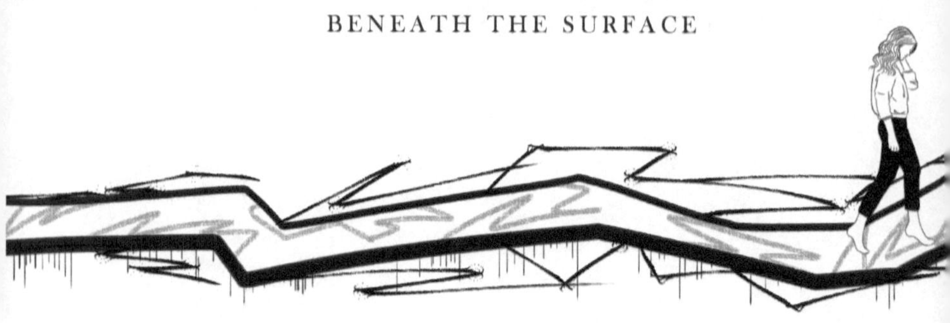

GPS: Road to Nowhere

Begin on Loneliness Avenue — keep moving forward. The road stretches endlessly, quiet except for the echo of your own footsteps. Soon, you'll reach the crossroads at Regret Road. Turn left, but tread carefully; the air grows heavier with each step, the weight of could-haves and should-haves pressing on your shoulders.

Before long, you'll find yourself winding through Insecurity Street. The path twists without warning, its uneven pavement catching your footing, reminding you that balance is fleeting here. Shadows loom large, distorting your sense of direction.

When you approach Fear Boulevard, take a right. Its cold winds bite at your skin, and the narrow stretch seems to close in on you. Don't linger too long — it's not a place for comfort, only survival.

A few blocks later, you'll stumble into Anxiety Alley, a chaotic side street that pulls you in without warning. Sharp corners, blind spots, and dead ends trap you in its maze. Your heartbeat races, echoing against the walls. Escape feels impossible, but if you manage it, you'll find yourself on Bitterness Lane.

At the roundabout, frustration sets in. Take the third exit onto

  LUCIANA FISHER

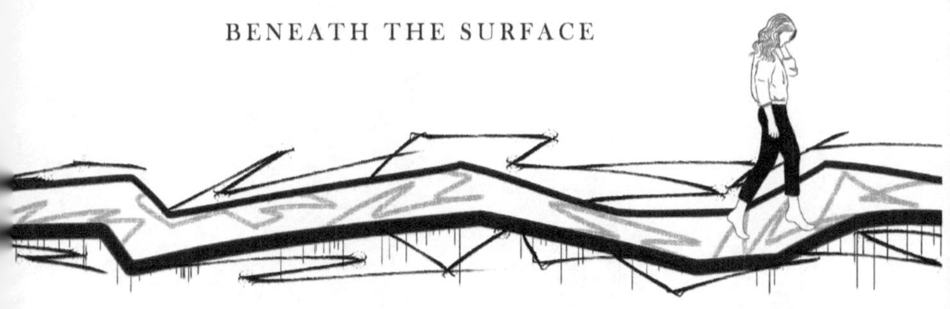

Frustration Drive. It loops endlessly, pulling you in circles until the world itself feels smaller, tighter. Don't lose focus — it's easy to forget why you even started this journey.

Eventually, you'll arrive at Grief Crossroad. A sharp left onto Desperation Way awaits, where the streetlights flicker weakly, offering little guidance. Doubt Circle looms ahead, its endless loops threatening to trap you in a spiral of second-guessing and self-blame.

Finally, you'll cross Rejection Bridge, where every step reverberates with the echoes of *not enough*. On the other side lies Hopelessness Square, the heart of this journey. Here, the roads diverge into bleak paths — Emptiness way, Resentment Road, or Guilt Place. None of them lead to salvation, only to darker corners.

And if the square is closed? There's no way forward, only a retreat to the roads you've already traveled — back through the loop again. But don't worry—all roads eventually lead to Isolation Street or Resentment Avenue, also known as the Roads to Nowhere — *unless you choose to break the cycle.*

Change the destination.

Trust your inner GPS. Let it guide you — a way out of the loop and onto the Road to Somewhere.

GPS: ROAD TO NOWHERE
BEHIND THE LINES:

GPS: Road to Nowhere is a deeply personal piece for me. As someone who has struggled with Complex Post-Traumatic Stress Disorder (CPTSD) and occasional bouts of depression, I have traveled every single one of the roads in this poem. Writing it was my way of giving voice to these experiences, mapping out the emotional labyrinth that so many of us navigate in silence.

Each street and intersection represent a mental state I've been trapped in—loneliness, insecurity, regret, and despair—capturing the endless loops that can feel impossible to escape. But this poem is not just about being lost; it's about finding the courage to trust your inner GPS and reroute toward healing, hope, and the possibility of a better path.

After nearly twenty years of therapy with Dr. G.—the best psychiatrist and a psychologist—years of medication management, and lots of writing, I am, for the most part, well and medication-free today. This poem reflects not only the struggles but also the resilience it takes to navigate those roads and break free from the cycles of pain.

Through this piece, I hope to connect with others who find themselves stuck in these loops, offering both validation and a gentle call to action. It's a reminder that while the Roads to Nowhere can feel endless, we have the power to change the destination. There's always a way out of the loop and onto the Road to Somewhere.

If you are experiencing bouts of depression, anxiety, or any of the feelings mentioned in this poem, please seek professional help—you don't have to navigate this journey alone.

U.S. National Suicide Prevention Lifeline: Dial 988

U.S Crisis Text Line: Text HOME to 741741

International Help: Find resources at <u>befrienders.org</u>

International Help: <u>https://www.iasp.info/suicidalthoughts</u>/

Reader Reflection:

Have you ever felt trapped in a cycle of negative thoughts or emotions? What steps might you take to trust your inner guidance and chart a new course toward healing and hope? (If you are struggling with any of the feelings mentioned in this poem, please consider seeking professional help)

GPS: Road to Somewhere

Start your journey on Hope Avenue—
walk with purpose until you reach Courage Road.
Take a right and feel the strength beneath your feet as you climb.
The path is steep, but each step rewards you with a deeper sense
of accomplishment.

Soon, you'll cross Patience Street—
keep steady; the bends are gentle but long.
Look around—the trees here are tall, offering shade and
moments to breathe.

At the next junction, merge onto Gratitude Lane—
the air is clearer here, the horizon wide and welcoming,
tinged with the scent of blooming flowers.
Each step lifts the weight of the past just a little more.

After a short distance, you'll meet Resilience Drive.

It may feel long, but each stretch strengthens your stride,
like a muscle that grows with every challenge you've overcome.

And as you leave Resilience Drive, you'll find Confidence
Boulevard.
Take a right. Stand tall—this road is paved with self-belief,
each stone laid by the moments you trusted your worth.
The path rises to meet you with every step.

Just ahead, you'll find Self-Acceptance Path—
a peaceful stretch where the burden of comparison dissolves.
Here, the wind is soft, carrying whispers of who you are.
You walk lighter, the weight of judgment falling away with each
step.

Take your time, and soon you'll meet Self-Esteem Street —
a road that feels like it lifts you with every step.
The ground beneath glows softly,
as though the street itself recognizes your worth.
Each step is a reminder that *you are enough*.

 LUCIANA FISHER

Cross Forgiveness Bridge —
its gentle arch spans waters rippling with past hurts.
Yet, the bridge feels weightless,
unburdening your steps and lightening your way forward.

Next, pass through Joy Circle —
a place where laughter comes easy, music fills the air,
inviting you to spin, to pause, and bask in happiness before
moving forward.

Ahead lies Acceptance Square,
where everything begins to feel whole,
where the pieces of your journey come together with ease.

At last, follow the signs to Peace Boulevard.
The road opens wide beneath a bright, endless sky,
guiding you effortlessly toward Happiness Square — you can't
miss it.
And as you arrive, you'll realize — the Journey was the destination all along.

GPS: ROAD TO SOMEWHERE
BEHIND THE LINES:

GPS: Road to Somewhere is a map of hope and self-discovery, inspired by my journey of navigating life's challenges and finding peace within myself. Writing this poem allowed me to reflect on the transformative process—the small, often difficult steps that lead to profound growth. Each road and intersection represent the qualities I've strived to cultivate, such as courage, patience, and self-acceptance, and the milestones I've encountered along the way.

This piece articulates the inner work needed for healing. Roads like "Resilience Drive" and "Forgiveness Bridge" symbolize the strength it takes to overcome obstacles and the liberation that comes from letting go of past hurts. Paths like "Self-Acceptance and Self-Esteem" remind us of the importance of embracing who we are, while "Joy Circle and Acceptance Square" highlight the moments of lightness and clarity we experience along the way.

Although my GPS is still faulty at times, I find myself

spending more time on these roads today. It's a reflection of my ongoing journey toward balance and fulfillment—proof that even with detours, we can find our way back to hope and healing.

Ultimately, this poem is a celebration of resilience and the beauty of the journey itself. It's a reminder that the destination isn't a physical place but a state of being—a sense of wholeness and peace that grows with every step forward. Through this piece, I hope to inspire readers to trust their own journeys, to see the challenges as part of their growth, and to recognize that every road, no matter how steep, leads to a place of fulfillment and strength.

Through this poem, I aim to share the message that even the most difficult journeys can lead to the light and that every step is a testament to our strength and growth.

Reader Reflection:

What roads have you traveled on your journey of growth and self-discovery? Which paths have challenged you, and which have brought you closer to peace and fulfillment? How might you trust your inner guidance to lead you to your 'Road to Somewhere'?

Again, Thank you.

As you turn the final page, I hope you remember this: life, much like poetry, is a journey of discovery, resilience, and connection. Each chapter and verse in this small collection of poems, offers a chance to reflect, grow, and find meaning in even the smallest moments.

No matter where you find yourself—whether navigating struggles or celebrating joyfully—know that every step holds the promise of transformation. You have the power to change direction, rewrite your story, and find beauty in the uniqueness of your journey.

I hope you enjoyed this deep dive *Behind the Lines* and into my creative process. These poems were not just written to be read but to be felt, explored, and shared. My hope was to spark a conversation with you, to connect through the words and emotions that fill these pages.

May these poems remind you to seek light in the shadows, find strength in vulnerability, and trust in the possibilities ahead. The road to somewhere is yours to create—one step, one word, one moment, one poem at a time.

Thank you for walking this path with me. May you continue to explore, dream, and live with a heart open to possibility and a soul filled with courage.

With gratitude,

Luciana Fisher

Did you enjoy this? I would love to hear from you. You can email me at: **hello@lucianafisher.com** or find me on IG: **@lbfisher**

Pour your heart out, wanderer of life,
Let vulnerability be your compass, your guide,
For it is in sharing the depths of our soul,
That we find connections that make us whole.
-L.F.

What Readers Are Feeling

I absolutely loved reading your book! the structure is amazing. The way each poem is followed by a deep reflection and then a self-reflection section — it's such a unique setup. It allows the reader to process and appreciate the poetry in a whole new way. I've never read a book like this before, and i think it's brilliant!

— SHLEY ANGSTADT

Luciana opens a door wide enough to enter the whole of a life. There is a bioluminescence to her autobiographical rendering — her glow pulls you into the dark essence around it: joyfully tragic in some instances. This book isn't just poetry; it's a masterclass in storytelling, guiding reflections, and a nonlinear lattice of memory and legacy. It educates and elevates.

— ALEEM ABDAL-KHAALIQ

I was swept away on my own emotional journey while reading about your own. You are courageous through vulnerability, and you inspired me, as you will everyone who reads your words. I especially enjoyed the interactive component of the book because it creates an intimacy between you and the reader. Genius really! yours is not *just* a book of poetry, but an experience of poetry. congratulations, Luciana.

— SUSAN BRUMEL

Standard Address Number (SAN): 994-3277
ISBN: 979-8-9992954-0-8

Luciana Fisher's
Beneath the Surface Fund
for Survivorship & Neurodivergence

A portion of net revenue from each qualifying sale supports breast cancer and dyslexia/ neurodivergence causes in perpetuity, as outlined in Luciana Fisher LLC's legally binding Operating Agreement.

Made in the United States
West New York, NJ
21 June 2025